Plant Based Breakfast Cookbook for Beginners

Easy-to-Make and Low-Carb Breakfast and
Smoothies Recipes for Your Plant Based Lifestyle

Jennifer Smith

2

By reading this document, the reader agrees that under no circumstances is the author responsible for any losses, direct or indirect, which are incurred as a result of the use of information contained within this document, including, but not limited to, — errors, omissions, or inaccuracies

Table of Contents

RECIPES

Avocado and 'Sausage' Breakfast Sandwich

Preparation time: 15 minutes

Cooking Time 2 minutes

Servings 1

Ingredients

- 1 vegan sausage patty
- 1 cup kale, chopped
- 2 teaspoons extra virgin olive oil
- 1 tablespoon pepitas
- Salt and pepper, to taste
- 1 tablespoon vegan mayo
- 1/8 teaspoon chipotle powder
- 1 teaspoon jalapeno chopped
- 1 English muffin, toasted
- ¼ avocado, sliced

Directions:

1. Place a sauté pan over a high heat and add a drop of oil.
2. Add the vegan patty and Cooking Time: for 2 minutes.
3. Flip the patty then add the kale and pepitas.
4. Season well then Cooking Time: for another few minutes until the patty is cooked.

5. Find a small bowl and add the mayo, chipotle powder and the jalapeno. Stir well to combine.
6. Place the muffin onto a flat surface, spread with the spicy may then top with the patty.
7. Add the sliced avocado then serve and enjoy.

Nutrition:

Calories 571, Total Fat 42.3g, Saturated Fat 10.1g, Cholesterol 36mg, Sodium 1334mg, Total Carbohydrate 38.6g, Dietary Fiber 6.6g, Total Sugars 3.7g, Protein 14.4g, Calcium 193mg

Black Bean Breakfast Burritos

Preparation time: 30 minutes

Cooking Time 10 minutes

Servings 4

Ingredients

- ¾ cup white rice
- 1 ½ cups water
- ¼ teaspoon sea salt
- ½ lime, juiced
- ¼ cup fresh cilantro, chopped
- 4 small red potatoes, cut into bite-sized pieces
- ½ red onion, sliced into rings
- 1-2 tablespoons olive oil
- Salt & pepper, to taste
- 1 cup cooked black beans
- ¼ teaspoon each ground cumin garlic powder, and chili powder
- Salt & pepper, to taste
- ¼ ripe avocado
- 1 lime, juiced
- 1 cup purple cabbage, thinly sliced
- 1 jalapeno, seeds removed, thinly sliced
- Pinch salt and black pepper

- 2 large vegan flour tortillas white or wheat
- ½ ripe avocado sliced
- ¼ cup salsa
- Hot sauce

Directions:

1. Place the rice, water and salt in a pan and bring to the boil.
2. Cover and Cooking Time: on low until fluffy then remove from the heat and pop to one side.
3. Place a skillet over a medium heat, add 1-2 tablespoons olive oil and add the potatoes and onion.
4. Season well then leave to Cooking Time: for 10 minutes, stirring often.
5. Remove from the heat and pop to one side.
6. Take a small pan then add the beans, cumin, garlic and chili. Stir well.
7. Pop over a medium heat and bring to simmer. Reduce the heat to keep warm.
8. Take a small bowl and add the avocado and lime. Mash together.
9. Add the cabbage and jalapeno and stir well.

Season then pop to one side.

10.   Grab the cooked rice and add the lime juice and cilantro then toss with a fork.

11.   Gently warm the tortillas in a microwave for 10-20 seconds then add the fillings.

12.   Roll up, serve and enjoy.

Nutrition:

Calories 588, Total Fat 17.1g, Saturated Fat 3.4g, Sodium 272mg, Total Carbohydrate 94.8g, Dietary Fiber 16.2g, Total Sugars 5g, Protein 18.1g, Calcium 115mg, Iron 6mg, Potassium 1964mg

Oatmeal & Peanut Butter Breakfast Bar

Preparation time: 10 minutes

Cooking Time 0 minutes

Servings 8

Ingredients

- 1½ cups date, pit removed
- ½ cup peanut butter
- ½ cup old-fashioned rolled oats

Directions:

1. Grease and line an 8" x 8" baking tin with parchment and pop to one side.
2. Grab your food processor, add the dates and whizz until chopped.
3. Add the peanut butter and the oats and pulse.
4. Scoop into the baking tin then pop into the fridge or freezer until set.
5. Serve and enjoy.

Nutrition:

Calories 459, Total Fat 8.9g, Saturated Fat 1.8g, Cholesterol 0mg, Sodium 77mg, Total Carbohydrate 98.5g, Dietary Fiber 11.3g, Total Sugars 79.1g, Protein 7.7g, Calcium 51mg, Potassium 926mg

Chocolate Chip Banana Pancake

Preparation time: 15 minutes

Cooking Time 3 minutes

Servings 6

Ingredients

- 1 large ripe banana, mashed
- 2 tablespoons coconut sugar
- 3 tablespoons coconut oil, melted
- 1 cup coconut milk
- 1 ½ cups whole wheat flour
- 1 teaspoon baking soda
- ½ cup vegan chocolate chips
- Olive oil, for frying

Directions:

1. Grab a large bowl and add the banana, sugar, oil and milk. Stir well.
2. Add the flour and baking soda and stir again until combined.
3. Add the chocolate chips and fold through then pop to one side.
4. Place a skillet over a medium heat and add a drop of oil.
5. Pour ¼ of the batter into the pan and move the

pan to cover.

6. Cooking Time: for 3 minutes then flip and Cooking Time: on the other side.

7. Repeat with the remaining pancakes then serve and enjoy.

Nutrition:

Calories 315, Total Fat 18.2g, Saturated Fat 15.1g, Cholesterol 0mg, Sodium 221mg, Total Carbohydrate 35.2g, Dietary Fiber 2.6g, Total Sugars 8.2g, Protein 4.7g, Potassium 209mg

Gingerbread Waffles

Preparation time: 30minutes

Cooking Time 20 minutes

Servings 6

Ingredients

- 1 slightly heaping cup spelt flour
- 1 tablespoon ground flax seeds
- 2 teaspoons baking powder
- ¼ teaspoon baking soda
- ¼ teaspoon salt
- 1 ½ teaspoons ground cinnamon
- 2 teaspoons ground ginger
- 4 tablespoons coconut sugar
- 1 cup non-dairy milk
- 1 tablespoon apple cider vinegar
- 2 tablespoons black strap molasses
- 1½ tablespoons olive oil

Directions:

1. Find your waffle iron, oil generously and preheat.
2. Find a large bowl and add the dry ingredients. Stir well together.
3. Put the wet ingredients into another bowl and

18

stir until combined.

4. Add the wet to dry then stir until combined.

5. Pour the mixture into the waffle iron and Cooking Time: on a medium temperature for 20 minutes

6. Open carefully and remove.

7. Serve and enjoy.

Nutrition:

Calories 256, Total Fat 14.2g, Saturated Fat 2g, Cholesterol 0mg, Sodium 175mg, Total Carbohydrate 31.2g, Dietary Fiber 3.4g, Total Sugars 13.2g, Protein 4.2g, Calcium 150mg, Iron 2mg, Potassium 369mg

Blueberry French Toast Breakfast Muffins

Preparation time: 55 minutes

Cooking Time 25 minutes

Servings 12

Ingredients

- 1 cup unsweetened plant milk
- 1 tablespoon ground flaxseed
- 1 tablespoon almond meal
- 1 tablespoon maple syrup
- 1 teaspoon vanilla extract
- 1 teaspoon cinnamon
- 2 teaspoons nutritional yeast
- ¾ cup frozen blueberries
- 9 slices soft bread
- ¼ cup oats
- 1/3 cup raw pecans
- ¼ cup coconut sugar
- 3 tablespoons coconut butter, at room temperature
- 1/8 teaspoon sea salt
- 9 slices bread, each cut into 4

Directions:

1. Preheat your oven to 375°F and grease a

muffin tin. Pop to one side.

2. Find a medium bowl and add the flax, almond meal, nutritional yeast, maple syrup, milk, vanilla and cinnamon.

3. Mix well using a fork then pop into the fridge.

4. Grab your food processor and add the topping ingredients (except the coconut butter.Whizz to combine.

5. Add the butter then whizz again.

6. Grab your muffin tin and add a teaspoon of the flax and cinnamon batter to the bottom of each space.

7. Add a square of the bread then top with 5-6 blueberries.

8. Sprinkle with 2 teaspoons of the crumble then top with another piece of bread.

9. Place 5-6 more blueberries over the bread, sprinkle with more of the topping then add the other piece of bread.

10.   Add a tablespoon of the flax and cinnamon mixture over the top and add a couple of blueberries on the top.

11.   Pop into the oven and Cooking Time: for

25-25 minutes until the top begins to brown.

12.   Serve and enjoy.

Nutrition:

Calories 228, Total Fat 14.4g, Saturated Fat 5.1g, Cholesterol 0mg, Sodium 186mg, Total Carbohydrate 22.9g, Dietary Fiber 4g, Total Sugars 7.8g, Protein 4.3g, Calcium 87mg, Iron 2mg, Potassiuminutes

Greek Garbanzo Beans on Toast

Preparation time: 30 minutes

Cooking Time 5 minutes

Servings 2

Ingredients

- 2 tablespoons olive oil
- 3 small shallots, finely diced
- 2 large garlic cloves, finely diced
- ¼ teaspoon smoked paprika
- ½ teaspoon sweet paprika
- ½ teaspoon cinnamon
- ½ teaspoon salt
- ½-1 teaspoon sugar, to taste
- Black pepper, to taste
- 1 x 6 oz. can peel plum tomatoes
- 2 cups cooked garbanzo beans
- 4 slices of crusty bread, toasted
- Fresh parsley and dill
- Pitted Kalamata olives

Directions:

1. Pop a skillet over a medium heat and add the oil.
2. Add the shallots to the pan and Cooking Time:

for five minutes until soft.

3. Add the garlic and Cooking Time: for another minute then add the other spices to the pan.
4. Stir well then add the tomatoes.
5. Turn down the heat and simmer on low until the sauce thickens.
6. Add the garbanzo beans and warm through.
7. Season with the sugar, salt and pepper then serve and enjoy.

Nutrition:

Calories 1296, Total Fat 47.4g, Saturated Fat 8.7g, Cholesterol 11mg, Sodium 1335mg, Total Carbohydrate 175.7g, Dietary Fiber 36.3g, Total Sugars 25.4g, Protein 49.8g, Calcium 313mg, Iron 17mg, Potassium 1972mg

Sundried Tomato & Asparagus Quiche

Preparation time: 1 hour 20 minutes

Cooking Time 40 minutes

Servings 8

Ingredients

- 1 ½ cup all-purpose flour
- ½ teaspoon salt
- ½ cup vegan butter
- 2-3 tablespoons ice cold water
- 1 tablespoon coconut or vegetable oil
- ¼ cup white onion, minced
- 1 cup fresh asparagus, chopped
- 3 tablespoons dried tomatoes, chopped
- 1 x 14 oz. block medium/firm tofu, drained
- 3 tablespoons nutritional yeast
- 1 tablespoon non-dairy milk
- 1 tablespoon all-purpose flour
- 1 teaspoon dehydrated minced onion
- 2 teaspoons fresh lemon juice
- 1 teaspoon spicy mustard
- ½ teaspoon sea salt
- ½ teaspoon turmeric
- ½ teaspoon liquid smoke

- 3 tablespoons fresh basil, chopped
- 1/3 cup vegan mozzarella cheese
- Salt and pepper, to taste

Directions:

1. Preheat your oven to 350°F and grease 4 x 5" quiche pans and pop to one side.
2. Grab a medium bowl and add the flour and salt. Stir well.
3. Then cut the butter into chunks and add to the flour, rubbing into the flour with your fingers until it resembles breadcrumbs.
4. Add the water and roll together.
5. Roll out and place into the quiche pans.
6. Bake for 10 minutes then remove from the oven and pop to one side.
7. Place a skillet over a medium heat, add the oil and then add the onions.
8. Cooking Time: for five minutes until soft.
9. Throw in the asparagus and tomatoes and Cooking Time: for 5 more minutes. Remove from the heat and pop to one side.
10. Grab your food processor and add the tofu, nutritional yeast, milk, flour, onions,

turmeric, liquid smoke, lemon juice and salt.

11.   Whizz until smooth and pour into a bowl.

12.   Add the asparagus mixture, the basil and the cheese and stir well.

13.   Season with salt and pepper.

14.   Spoon into the pie crusts and pop back into the oven for 15-20 minutes until set and cooked through.

15.   Remove from the oven, leave to cool for 20 minutes then serve and enjoy.

Nutrition:

Calories 175, Total Fat 5.1g, Saturated Fat 2.3g, Cholesterol 1mg, Sodium 286mg, Total Carbohydrate 24.2g, Dietary Fiber 2.7g, Total Sugars 1.2g, Protein 9.4g, Calcium 118mg, Iron 3mg, Potassium 252mg

Smoky Sweet Potato Tempeh Scramble

Preparation time: 17 minutes

Cooking Time 13 minutes

Servings 8

Ingredients

- 2 tablespoons olive oil
- 1 small sweet potato, finely diced
- 1 small onion, diced
- 2 garlic cloves, minced
- 8 oz. package tempeh, crumbled
- 1 small red bell pepper, diced
- 1 tablespoon soy sauce
- 1 tablespoon ground cumin
- 1 tablespoon smoked paprika
- 1 tablespoon maple syrup
- Juice of ½ lemon
- 1 avocado, sliced
- 2 scallions, chopped
- 4 tortillas
- 2 tbsp. Hot sauce

Directions:

1. Place a skillet over a medium heat and add the oil.

2. Add the sweet potato and Cooking Time: for five minutes until getting soft.
3. Add the onion and Cooking Time: for another five minutes until soft.
4. Stir through the garlic and Cooking Time: for a minute.
5. Add the tempeh, pepper, soy, cumin, paprika, maple and lemon juice and Cooking Time: for two more minutes.
6. Serve with the optional extras then enjoy.

Nutrition:

Calories 200, Total Fat 12.3g, Saturated Fat 2.2g, Cholesterol 0mg, Sodium 224mg, Total Carbohydrate 19g, Dietary Fiber 3.7g, Total Sugars 6.5g, Protein 7.5g, Calcium 64mg, Iron 2mg, Potassium 430mg

Cinnamon Rolls with Cashew Frosting

Preparation time: 30 minutes

Cooking Time 25 minutes

Servings 12

Ingredients

- 3 tablespoons vegan butter
- ¾ cup unsweetened almond milk
- ½ teaspoon salt
- 3 tablespoons caster sugar
- 1 teaspoon vanilla extract
- ½ cup pumpkin puree
- 3 cups all-purpose flour
- 2 ¼ teaspoons dried active yeast
- 3 tablespoons softened vegan butter
- 3 tablespoons brown sugar
- ½ teaspoon cinnamon
- ½ cup cashews, soaked 1 hour in boiling water
- ½ cup icing sugar
- 1 teaspoon vanilla extract
- 2/3 cup almond milk

Directions:

1. Grease a baking sheet and pop to one side.
2. Find a small bowl, add the butter and pop into

the microwave to melt.

3. Add the sugar and stir well then set aside to cool.

4. Grab a large bowl and add the flour, salt and yeast. Stir well to mix together.

5. Place the cooled butter into a jug, add the pumpkin puree, vanilla and almond milk. Stir well together.

6. Pour the wet ingredients into the dry and stir well to combine.

7. Tip onto a flat surface and knead for 5 minutes, adding extra flour as needed to avoid sticking.

8. Pop back into the bowl, cover with plastic wrap and pop into the fridge overnight.

9. Next morning, remove the dough from the fridge and punch down with your fingers.

10.   Using a rolling pin, roll to form an 18" rectangle then spread with butter.

11.   Find a small bowl and add the sugar and cinnamon. Mix well then sprinkle with the butter.

12.   Roll the dough into a large sausage then slice into sections.

13.   Place onto the greased baking sheet and leave in a dark place to rise for one hour.

14.   Preheat the oven to 350°F.

15.   Meanwhile, drain the cashews and add them to your blender. Whizz until smooth.

16.   Add the sugar and the vanilla then whizz again.

17.   Add the almond milk until it reaches your desired consistency.

18.   Pop into the oven and bake for 20 minutes until golden.

19.   Pour the glaze over the top then serve and enjoy.

Nutrition:

Calories 226, Total Fat 6.5g, Saturated Fat 3.4g, Cholesterol 0mg, Sodium 113mg, Total Carbohydrate 38g, Dietary Fiber 1.9g, Total Sugars 11.3g, Protein 4.9g, Calcium 34mg, Iron 2mg, Potassium 153mg

No-Bake Chewy Granola Bars

Preparation time: 10 minutes

Cooking Time 10 minutes

Servings 8

Ingredients

- ¼ cup coconut oil
- ¼ cup honey or maple syrup
- ¼ teaspoon salt
- 1 teaspoon vanilla extract
- ½ teaspoon cardamominutes
- ¼ teaspoon cinnamon
- Pinch of nutmeg
- 1 cup old-fashioned oats
- ½ cup sliced raw almonds
- ¼ cup sunflower seeds
- ¼ cup pumpkin seeds
- 1 tablespoon chia seeds
- 1 cup chopped dried figs

Directions:

1. Line a 6" x 8" baking dish with parchment paper and pop to one side.
2. Grab a saucepan and add the oil, honey, salt and spices.

3. Pop over a medium heat and stir until it melts together.
4. Reduce the heat, add the oats and stir to coat.
5. Add the seeds, nuts and dried fruit and stir through again.
6. Cooking Time: for 10 minutes.
7. Remove from the heat and transfer the oat mixture to the pan.
8. Press down until it's packed firm.
9. Leave to cool completely then cut into 8 bars.
10.   Serve and enjoy.

Nutrition:

Calories 243, Total Fat 13.3g, Saturated Fat 6.7g, Cholesterol 0mg, Sodium 78mg, Total Carbohydrate 30.8g, Dietary Fiber 4.3g, Total Sugars 21.1g, Protein 4.2g, Calcium 67mg, Iron 2mg, Potassium 285mg

Hot Sausage and Pepper Breakfast Casserole

Preparation time: 57 minutes

Cooking Time 50 minutes

Servings 8

Ingredients

- 10 cup white bread, cubed
- 2¾ cups ice water
- 1 ¼ cup plant-based unsweetened creamer
- 2 tablespoons extra-virgin olive oil
- 3 vegan sausage, sliced
- 1 bell pepper, seeded and chopped
- 1 medium onion, chopped
- 2 garlic cloves, minced
- 5 cups spinach leaves
- 1 cup vegan parmesan, grated
- 1 teaspoon ground sea salt, or to taste
- ½ teaspoon ground nutmeg
- ½ teaspoon ground black pepper
- 1 tablespoon fresh parsley, chopped
- 1 teaspoon fresh rosemary, chopped
- 1 teaspoon fresh thyme, chopped
- 1 teaspoon fresh oregano, chopped
- 1 tablespoon vegan butter

Directions:

1. Preheat your oven to 375°F and grease a 13" x 8" baking dish.
2. Grab a medium bowl and add the water, milk and nutmeg. Whisk well until combined.
3. Pop a skillet over a medium heat and add the oil.
4. Add the sausage to the pan and Cooking Time: for 8-10 minutes until browned. Remove from the pan and pop to one side.
5. Add the onions and Cooking Time: for 3 minutes.
6. Add the peppers and Cooking Time: for 5 minutes.
7. Add the garlic, salt and pepper and Cooking Time: for 2 minutes then remove from the pan and pop to one side.
8. Add the spinach to the pan and Cooking Time: until wilted.
9. Remove the spinach from the pan then chop. Squeeze out the water.
10. Grab the greased baking dish and add half the cubed bread to the bottom.

11.   Add half the spinach to the top followed by half the spinach and half of the onion and pepper mixture.

12.   Sprinkle with half the parmesan then repeat.

13.   Whisk the egg mixture again then pour over the casserole.

14.   Pop into the oven and bake for 30 minutes until browned.

15.   Serve and enjoy.

Nutrition:

Calories 263, Total Fat 8.2g, Saturated Fat 1g, Cholesterol 0mg, Sodium 673mg, Total Carbohydrate 31.8g, Dietary Fiber 3.4g, Total Sugars 3.6g, Protein 12.9g, Calcium 239mg, Iron 3mg, Potassium 377mg

Easy Hummus Toast

Preparation time: 10 minutes

Cooking Time 0 minutes

Servings 1

Ingredients

- 2 slices sprouted wheat bread
- ¼ cup hummus
- 1 tablespoon hemp seeds
- 1 tablespoon roasted unsalted sunflower seeds

Directions:

1. Start by toasting your bread.
2. Top with the hummus and seeds then eat!

Nutrition:

Calories 445, Total Fat 16.3g, Saturated Fat 2.2g, Cholesterol 0mg, Sodium 597mg, Total Carbohydrate 54.5g, Dietary Fiber 10.5g, Total Sugars 6.1g, Protein 22.6g, Calcium 116mg, Iron 6mg, Potassium 471mg

Fluffy Garbanzo Bean Omelet

Preparation time: 20 minutes

Cooking Time 7 minutes

Servings 2

Ingredients

- ¼ cup besan flour
- 1 tablespoon nutritional yeast
- ½ teaspoon baking powder
- ¼ teaspoon turmeric
- ½ teaspoon chopped chives
- ¼ teaspoon garlic powder
- 1/8 teaspoon black pepper
- ½ teaspoon Ener-G egg replacer
- ¼ cup water
- ½ cup Romaine Leafy Green Fresh Express
- ½ cup Veggies
- 1 tablespoon Salsa
- 1 tablespoon Ketchup
- 1 tablespoon Hot sauce
- 1 tablespoon Parsley

Directions:

1. Grab a medium bowl and combine all the ingredients except the greens and veggies.

Leave to stand for five minutes.

2. Place a skillet over a medium heat and add the oil.

3. Pour the batter into the pan, spread and Cooking Time: for 3-5 minutes until the edges pull away from the pan.

4. Add the greens and the veggies of your choice then fold the omelet over.

5. Cooking Time: for 2 more minutes then pop onto a plate.

6. Serve with the topping of your choice.

7. Serve and enjoy.

Nutrition:

Calories 104, Total Fat 1.3g, Saturated Fat 0.2g, Cholesterol 0mg, Sodium 419mg, Total Carbohydrate 17.9g, Dietary Fiber 4.6g, Total Sugars 4.7g, Protein 6.6g, Calcium 69mg, Iron 3mg, Potassium 423mg

Cardamom & Blueberry Oatmeal

Preparation time: 10 minutes

Cooking Time 3 minutes

Servings 1

Ingredients

- ¾ cup quick oats
- 1¼ cup water
- ½ cup unsweetened almond milk, divided
- 2 tablespoons pure maple syrup
- ¼ heaping teaspoon cinnamon
- 1/8 teaspoon cardamominutes
- Handful walnuts
- Handful dried currants

Directions:

1. Place the water into a small saucepan and bring to the boil.
2. Add the oats, stir through, reduce the heat to medium and Cooking Time: for 3 minutes.
3. Add half of the milk, stir again and Cooking Time: for another few seconds.
4. Remove from the heat and leave to stand for 3 minutes.
5. Transfer to a bowl and to with the remaining

ingredients.

6. Drizzle with the milk then serve and enjoy.

Nutrition:

Calories 568, Total Fat 24.4g, Saturated Fat 1.9g, Cholesterol 0mg, Sodium 118mg, Total Carbohydrate 77g, Dietary Fiber 10.4g, Total Sugars 26.8g, Protein 16.5g, Vitamin D 1mcg, Calcium 263mg, Iron 5mg, Potassium 651mg

Cashew Cheese Spread

Preparation Time: 5 minutes

Cooking Time: 0 minutes

Servings: 5

Ingredients:

- 1 cup water
- 1 cup raw cashews
- 1 tsp. nutritional yeast
- ½ tsp. salt

Optional: 1 tsp. garlic powder

Directions:

1. Soak the cashews for 6 hours in water.
2. Drain and transfer the soaked cashews to a food processor.
3. Add 1 cup of water and all the other ingredients and blend.
4. For the best flavor, serve chilled.
5. Enjoy immediately, or store for later.

Nutrition:

Calories 162, Total Fat 12.7g, Saturated Fat 2.5g, Cholesterol 0mg, Sodium 239mg, Total Carbohydrate 9.7g, Dietary Fiber 1.1g, Total Sugars 1.5g, Protein 4.6g, Calcium 15mg, Iron 2mg, Potassium 178mg

High Protein Peanut Butter Smoothie

Preparation time: 3 minutes

Servings: 2

Ingredients

- 2 cups kale
- 1 banana
- 2 tbsp. hemp seeds
- 1 tbsp. peanut butter
- 2/3 cup water
- 2 cups ice
- 1 cup almond or cashew milk
- 2 tbsp. cacao powder
- 1 scoop Vega vanilla protein powder

Directions:

1. Pop the kale and banana in a blender, then add the hemp seeds and peanut butter.
2. Add the milk, water and ice and blend until ingredients are combined.
3. Add the protein powder.
4. Pour into glasses and serve.

Nutrition:

Calories 687, Total Fat 50.4g, Saturated Fat 38g, Cholesterol 0mg, Sodium 176mg, Total Carbohydrate

46.5g, Dietary Fiber 9.9g, Total Sugars 23.7g, Protein 20.4g, Vitamin D 0mcg, Calcium 150mg, Iron 8mg, Potassium 979mg

Pineapple and Kale Smoothie

Preparation time: 3 minutes

Servings 2

Ingredients

- 1 cup Greek yogurt
- 1½ cups cubed pineapple
- 3 cups baby kale
- 1 cucumber
- 2 tbsp, hemp seeds

Directions:

1. Pop everything in a blender and blitz
2. Pour into glasses and serve.

Nutrition:

Calories 509, Total Fat 8.9g, Saturated Fat 3.3g, Cholesterol 10mg, Sodium 127mg, Total Carbohydrate 87.1g, Dietary Fiber 10.3g, Total Sugars 55.3g, Protein 30.6g, Vitamin D 0mcg, Calcium 438mg, Iron 5mg, Potassium 1068mg

Vanilla and Almond Smoothie

Preparation time: 3 minutes

Servings 1

Ingredients

- 2 scoops vegan vanilla protein powder
- ½ cup almonds
- 1 cup water

Directions:

1. Pop everything in a blender and blitz
2. Pour into glasses and serve.

Nutrition:

Calories 415, Total Fat 33.8g, Saturated Fat 1.8g, Cholesterol 0mg, Sodium 108mg, Total Carbohydrate 18.2g, Dietary Fiber 7.9g, Total Sugars 2g, Protein 42.1g, Vitamin D 0mcg, Calcium 255mg, Iron 9mg, Potassium 351mg

Berry Blast Smoothie

Preparationtime:3minutes

Servings: 2

Ingredients

- 1 cup raspberries
- 1 cup frozen blueberries
- 1 cup frozen blackberries
- 1 cup almond milk
- ¼ cup Soy Yogurt

Directions:

1. Pop everything in a blender and blitz
2. Pour into glasses and serve.

Nutrition:

Calories 404, Total Fat 30.4g, Saturated Fat 25.5g, Cholesterol 0mg, Sodium 22mg, Total Carbohydrate 34.5g, Dietary Fiber 12.5g, Total Sugars 19.6g, Protein 6.3g, Vitamin D 0mcg, Calcium 112mg, Iron 4mg, Potassium 581mg

Greens and Berry Smoothie

Preparation time: 3 minutes

Servings 2

Ingredients

- 1 cup frozen berries
- 1 cup kale or spinach
- ¾ cup milk almond, oat or coconut milk
- ½ tbsp chia seeds

Directions:

1. Pop everything in a blender and blitz
2. Pour into glasses and serve.

Nutrition:

Calories 298, Saturated Fat 19.3g, Cholesterol 0mg, Sodium 29mg, Total Carbohydrate 20g, Dietary Fiber 7.4g, Total Sugars 8g, Protein 4.7g, Vitamin D 0mcg, Calcium 114mg, Iron 3mg, Potassium 520mg

Peanut Butter Banana Quinoa Bowl

Preparation time: 15 minutes

Cooking time: 15 minutes

Servings: 1

Ingredients:

- 175ml unsweetened soy milk
- 85g uncooked quinoa
- ½ teaspoon Ceylon cinnamon
- 10g chia seeds
- 30g organic peanut butter
- 30ml unsweetened almond milk
- 10g raw cocoa powder
- 5 drops liquid stevia
- 1 small banana, peeled, sliced

Directions:

1. In a saucepan, bring soy milk, quinoa, and Ceylon cinnamon to a boil.
2. Reduce heat and simmer 15 minutes.
3. Remove from the heat and stir in Chia seeds. Cover the saucepan with lid and place aside for 15 minutes.
4. In the meantime, microwave peanut butter and almond milk for 30 seconds on high. Remove

and stir until runny. Repeat the process if needed.

5. Stir in raw cocoa powder and Stevia.
6. To serve; fluff the quinoa with fork and transfer in a bowl.
7. Top with sliced banana.
8. Drizzle the quinoa with peanut butter.
9. Serve.

Nutrition:

Calories 718

Total Fat 29.6g

Total Carbohydrate 90.3g

Dietary Fiber 17.5g

Total Sugars 14.5g

Protein 30.4g

Orange Pumpkin Pancakes

Preparation time: 10 minutes

Cooking time: 15 minutes

Servings: 4

Ingredients:

- 10g ground flax meal
- 45ml water
- 235ml unsweetened soy milk
- 15ml lemon juice
- 60g buckwheat flour
- 60g all-purpose flour
- 8g baking powder, aluminum-free
- 2 teaspoons finely grated orange zest
- 25g white chia seeds
- 120g organic pumpkin puree (or just bake the pumpkin and puree the flesh
- 30ml melted and cooled coconut oil
- 5ml vanilla paste
- 30ml pure maple syrup

Directions:

1. Combine ground flax meal with water in a small bowl. Place aside for 10 minutes.
2. Combine almond milk and cider vinegar in a

medium bowl. Place aside for 5 minutes.

3. In a separate large bowl, combine buckwheat flour, all-purpose flour, baking powder, orange zest, and chia seeds.

4. Pour in almond milk, along with pumpkin puree, coconut oil, vanilla, and maple syrup.

5. Whisk together until you have a smooth batter.

6. Heat large non-stick skillet over medium-high heat. Brush the skillet gently with some coconut oil.

7. Pour 60ml of batter into skillet. Cooking Time: the pancake for 1 minute, or until bubbles appear on the surface.

8. Lift the pancake gently with a spatula and flip.

9. Cooking Time: 1 ½ minutes more. Slide the pancake onto a plate. Repeat with the remaining batter.

10.   Serve warm.

Nutrition:

Calories 301

Total Fat 12.6g

Total Carbohydrate 41.7g

Dietary Fiber 7.2g

Total Sugars 9.9g

Protein 8.1g

Chilled Cantaloupe Smoothie

Preparation time: 10 minutes

Servings 2

Ingredients:

- 1½ cups cantaloupe, diced
- 2 Tbsp frozen orange juice concentrate
- ¼ cup white wine
- 2 ice cubes
- 1 Tbsp lemon juice
- ½ cup Mint leaves, for garnish

Directions:

1. Blend all ingredients to create a smooth mixture.
2. Top with mint leaves, and serve.

Nutrition:

Calories 349, Total Fat 13.1g, Saturated Fat 11.3g, Cholesterol 0mg, Sodium 104mg, Total Carbohydrate 50.5g, Dietary Fiber 5.5g, Total Sugars 46.4g, Protein 6.5g, Vitamin D 0mcg, Calcium 117mg, Iron 5mg, Potassium 1320mg

Sweet Potato Slices With Fruits

Preparation time: 10 minutes

Cooking time: 10 minutes

Servings: 2

Ingredients:

The base:

- 1 sweet potato

Topping:

- 60g organic peanut butter
- 30ml pure maple syrup
- 4 dried apricots, sliced
- 30g fresh raspberries

Directions:

1. Peel and cut sweet potato into ½ cm thick slices.
2. Place the potato slices in a toaster on high for 5 minutes. Toast your sweet potatoes TWICE.
3. Arrange sweet potato slices onto a plate.
4. Spread the peanut butter over sweet potato slices.
5. Drizzle the maple syrup over the butter.
6. Top each slice with an equal amount of sliced apricots and raspberries.

7. Serve.

Nutrition:

Calories 300

Total Fat 16.9g

Total Carbohydrate 32.1g

Dietary Fiber 6.2g

Total Sugars 17.7g

Protein 10.3g

Choc-Banana Smoothie

Preparationtime:3minutes

Servings: 2

Ingredients

- 1 banana
- 2 tbsp. hemp seeds
- 2/3 cup water
- 2 cups ice
- 1 cup almond or cashew milk
- 2 scoop Vegan chocolate protein powder
- 2 tbsp. cacao powder

Directions:

1. Pop everything in a blender and blitz
2. Pour into glasses and serve.

Nutrition:

Calories 676, Total Fat 52.3g, Saturated Fat 38.1g, Cholesterol 0mg, Sodium 46mg, Total Carbohydrate 41.6g, Dietary Fiber 8.7g, Total Sugars 25.2g, Protein 22.4g, Vitamin D 0mcg, Calcium 80mg, Iron 6mg, Potassium 528mg

Spinach Tofu Scramble With Sour Cream

Preparation time: 10 minutes

Cooking time: 15 minutes

Servings: 2

Ingredients:

Sour cream:

- 75g raw cashews, soaked overnight
- 30ml lemon juice
- 5g nutritional yeast
- 60ml water
- 1 good pinch salt

Tofu scramble:

- 15ml olive oil
- 1 small onion, diced
- 1 clove garlic, minced
- 400 firm tofu, pressed, crumbled
- ½ teaspoon ground cumin
- ½ teaspoon curry powder
- ½ teaspoon turmeric
- 2 tomatoes, diced
- 30g baby spinach
- Salt, to taste

Directions:

1. Make the cashew sour cream; rinse and drain soaked cashews.
2. Place the cashews, lemon juice, nutritional yeast, water, and salt in a food processor.
3. Blend on high until smooth, for 5-6 minutes.
4. Transfer to a bowl and place aside.
5. Make the tofu scramble; heat olive oil in a skillet.
6. Add onion and Cooking Time: 5 minutes over medium-high.
7. Add garlic, and Cooking Time: stirring, for 1 minute.
8. Add crumbled tofu, and stir to coat with oil.
9. Add the cumin, curry, and turmeric. Cooking Time: the tofu for 2 minutes.
10. Add the tomatoes and Cooking Time: for 2 minutes.
11. Add spinach and cook, tossing until completely wilted, about 1 minute.
12. Transfer tofu scramble on the plate.
13. Top with a sour cream and serve.

Nutrition:

Calories 411

Total Fat 26.5g

Total Carbohydrate 23.1g

Dietary Fiber 5.9g

Total Sugars 6.3g

Protein 25g

Overnight Chia Oats

Preparation time: 15minutes + inactive time

Cooking time: 20 minutes

Servings: 4

Ingredients:

- 470ml full-fat soy milk
- 90g old-fashioned rolled oats
- 40g chia seeds
- 15ml pure maple syrup
- 25g crushed pistachios
- Blackberry Jam:
- 500g blackberries
- 45ml pure maple syrup
- 30ml water
- 45g chia seeds
- 15ml lemon juice

Directions:

1. Make the oats; in a large bowl, combine soy milk, oats, chia seeds, and maple syrup.
2. Cover and refrigerate overnight.
3. Make the jam; combine blackberries, maple syrup, and water in a saucepan.
4. Simmer over medium heat for 10 minutes.

5. Add the chia seeds and simmer the blackberries for 10 minutes.

6. Remove from heat and stir in lemon juice. Mash the blackberries with a fork and place aside to cool.

7. Assemble; divide the oatmeal among four serving bowls.

8. Top with each bowl blackberry jam.

9. Sprinkle with pistachios before serving.

Nutrition:

Calories 362

Total Fat 13.4g

Total Carbohydrate 52.6g

Dietary Fiber 17.4g

Total Sugars 24.6g

Protein 12.4g

Amaranth Quinoa Porridge

Preparation time: 5 minutes

Cooking time: 35 minutes

Servings: 2

Ingredients:

- 85g quinoa
- 70g amaranth
- 460ml water
- 115ml unsweetened soy milk
- ½ teaspoon vanilla paste
- 15g almond butter
- 30ml pure maple syrup
- 10g raw pumpkin seeds
- 10g pomegranate seeds

Directions:

1. Combine quinoa, amaranth, and water.
2. Bring to a boil over medium-high heat.
3. Reduce heat and simmer the grains, stirring occasionally, for 20 minutes.
4. Stir in milk and maple syrup.
5. Simmer for 6-7 minutes. Remove from the heat and stir in vanilla, and almond butter.
6. Allow the mixture to stand for 5 minutes.

7. Divide the porridge between two bowls.

8. Top with pumpkin seeds and pomegranate seeds.

9. Serve.

Nutrition:

Calories 474

Total Fat 13.3g

Total Carbohydrate 73.2g

Dietary Fiber 8.9g

Total Sugars 10g

Protein 17.8g

Cacao Lentil Muffins

Preparation time: 10 minutes

Cooking time: 15 minutes

Servings: 12 muffins (2 per serving

Ingredients:

- 195g cooked red lentils
- 50ml melted coconut oil
- 45ml pure maple syrup
- 60ml unsweetened almond milk
- 60ml water
- 60g raw cocoa powder
- 120g whole-wheat flour
- 20g peanut flour
- 10g baking powder, aluminum-free
- 70g Vegan chocolate chips

Directions:

1. Preheat oven to 200C/400F.
2. Line 12-hole muffin tin with paper cases.
3. Place the cooked red lentils in a food blender. Blend on high until smooth.
4. Transfer the lentils puree into a large bowl.
5. Stir in coconut oil, maple syrup, almond milk, and water.

6. In a separate bowl, whisk cocoa powder, whole-wheat flour, peanut flour, and baking powder.
7. Fold in liquid ingredients and stir until just combined.
8. Add chocolate chips and stir until incorporated.
9. Divide the batter among 12 paper cases.
10.   Tap the muffin tin gently onto the kitchen counter to remove air.
11.   Bake the muffins for 15 minutes.
12.   Cool muffins on a wire rack.
13.   Serve.

Nutrition:

Calories 372

Total Fat 13.5g

Total Carbohydrate 52.7g

Dietary Fiber 12.9g

Total Sugars 13g

Protein 13.7g

Breakfast Oat Brownies

Preparation time: 10 minutes

Cooking time: 40 minutes

Servings: 10 slices (2 per serving

Ingredients:

- 180g old-fashioned rolled oats
- 80g peanut flour
- 30g chickpea flour
- 25g flax seeds meal
- 5g baking powder, aluminum-free
- ½ teaspoon baking soda
- 5ml vanilla paste
- 460ml unsweetened vanilla soy milk
- 80g organic applesauce
- 55g organic pumpkin puree
- 45g organic peanut butter
- 5ml liquid stevia extract
- 25g slivered almonds

Directions:

1. Preheat oven to 180C/350F.
2. Line 18cm baking pan with parchment paper, leaving overhanging sides.
3. In a large bowl, combine oats, peanut flour,

chickpea flour, flax seeds, baking powder, and baking soda.

4. In a separate bowl, whisk together vanilla paste, soy milk, applesauce. Pumpkin puree, peanut butter, and stevia.

5. Fold the liquid ingredients into dry ones and stir until incorporated.

6. Pour the batter into the prepared baking pan.

7. Sprinkle evenly with slivered almonds.

8. Bake the oat brownies for 40 minutes.

9. Remove from the oven and place aside to cool.

10.   Slice and serve.

Nutrition:

Calories 309

Total Fat 15.3g

Total Carbohydrate 32.2g

Dietary Fiber 9.2g

Total Sugars 9.1g

Protein 13.7g

Chickpea Crepes With Mushrooms And Spinach

Preparation time: 20 minutes + inactive time

Cooking time: 15 minutes

Servings: 4

Ingredients:

Crepes:

- 140g chickpea flour
- 30g peanut flour
- 5g nutritional yeast
- 5g curry powder
- 350ml water
- Salt, to taste

Filling:

- 10ml olive oil
- 4 portabella mushroom caps, thinly sliced
- 1 onion, thinly sliced
- 30g baby spinach
- Salt, and pepper, to taste

Vegan mayo:

- 60ml aquafaba
- 1/8 teaspoon cream of tartar
- ¼ teaspoon dry mustard powder
- 15ml lemon juice

- 5ml raw cider vinegar
- 15ml maple syrup
- 170ml avocado oil
- Salt, to taste

Directions:

1. Make the mayo; combine aquafaba, cream of tartar, mustard powder. Lemon juice, cider vinegar, and maple syrup in a bowl.
2. Beat with a hand mixer for 30 seconds.
3. Set the mixer to the highest speed. Drizzle in avocado oil and beat for 10 minutes or until you have a mixture that resembles mayonnaise.
4. Of you want paler (in the color mayoadd more lemon juice.
5. Season with salt and refrigerate for 1 hour.
6. Make the crepes; combine chickpea flour, peanut flour, nutritional yeast, curry powder, water, and salt to taste in a food blender.
7. Blend until smooth.
8. Heat large non-stick skillet over medium-high heat. Spray the skillet with some cooking oil.
9. Pour ¼ cup of the batter into skillet and with a swirl motion distribute batter all over the skillet

bottom.

10.   Cooking Time: the crepe for 1 minute per side. Slide the crepe onto a plate and keep warm.

11.   Make the filling; heat olive oil in a skillet over medium-high heat.

12.   Add mushrooms and onion and Cooking Time: for 6-8 minutes.

13.   Add spinach and toss until wilted, for 1 minute.

14.   Season with salt and pepper and transfer into a large bowl.

15.   Fold in prepared vegan mayo.

16.   Spread the prepared mixture over chickpea crepes. Fold gently and serve.

Nutrition:

Calories 428

Total Fat 13.3g

Total Carbohydrate 60.3g

Dietary Fiber 18.5g

Total Sugars 13.2g

Protein 22.6g

Mexican Breakfast

Preparation time: 10 minutes

Cooking time: 10 minutes

Servings: 4

Ingredients:

- 170g cherry tomatoes, halved
- 1 small red onion, chopped
- 25ml lime juice
- 50ml olive oil
- 1 clove garlic, minced
- 1 teaspoon red chili flakes
- 1 teaspoon ground cumin
- 700g can black beans* (or cooked beans), rinsed
- 4 slices whole-grain bread
- 1 avocado, peeled, pitted
- Salt, to taste

Directions:

1. Combine tomatoes, onion, lime juice, and 15ml olive oil in a bowl.
2. Season to taste and place aside.
3. Heat 2 tablespoons olive oil in a skillet.
4. Add onion and Cooking Time: 4 minutes over

medium-high heat.

5. Add garlic and Cooking Time: stirring for 1 minute.

6. Add red chili flakes and cumin. Cooking Time: for 30 seconds.

7. Add beans and Cooking Time: tossing gently for 2 minutes.

8. Stir in ¾ of the tomato mixture and season to taste.

9. Remove from heat.

10.   Slice the avocado very thinly.

11.   Spread the beans mixture over bread slices. Top with remaining tomato and sliced avocado.

12.   Serve.

Nutrition:

Calories 476

Total Fat 21.9g

Total Carbohydrate 52.4g

Dietary Fiber 19.5g

Total Sugars 5.3g

Protein 17.1g

Goji Breakfast Bowl

Preparation time: 10 minutes

Servings: 2

Ingredients:

- 15g chia seeds
- 10g buckwheat
- 15g hemp seeds
- 20g Goji berries
- 235mml vanilla soy milk

Directions:

1. Combine chia, buckwheat, hemp seeds, and Goji berries in a bowl.
2. Heat soy milk in a saucepan until start to simmer.
3. Pour the milk over "cereals".
4. Allow the cereals to stand for 5 minutes.
5. Serve.

Nutrition:

Calories 339

Total Fat 14.3g

Total Carbohydrate 41.8g

Dietary Fiber 10.5g

Total Sugars 20g

Protein 13.1g

Sweet Coffee and Cacao Smoothie

Preparation time: 3 minutes

Servings 2

Ingredients

- 2 tsp Coffee
- ½ a Banana
- 1 cup Almond Milk
- 1 tsp Cashew Butter
- 2 tsp Cacao Powder
- 1 tsp maple Syrup
- 1 scoop vegan protein powder
- ½ cup Chocolate

Directions:

1. Pop everything in a blender and blitz
2. Pour into glasses and serve.

Nutrition:

Calories 614, Total Fat 43.2g, Saturated Fat 34.6g, Cholesterol 10mg, Sodium 146mg, Total Carbohydrate 44.7g, Dietary Fiber 5.4g, Total Sugars 31.2g, Protein 17.6g, Vitamin D 0mcg, Calcium 104mg, Iron 4mg, Potassium 614mg

Creamy Chocolate Shake

Preparation time: 10 minutes

Servings 2

Ingredients:

- 2 frozen ripe bananas, chopped
- 1/3 cup frozen strawberries
- 2 tbsp cocoa powder
- 2 tbsp salted almond butter
- 2 cups unsweetened vanilla almond milk
- 1 dash Stevia or agave nectar
- 1/3 cup ice

Directions:

1. Add all ingredients in a blender and blend until smooth.
2. Take out and serve.

Nutrition:

Calories 272, Total Fat 14.3g, Saturated Fat 1.5g, Cholesterol 0mg, Sodium 315mg, Total Carbohydrate 37g, Dietary Fiber 7.3g, Total Sugars 16.8g, Protein 6.2g, Vitamin D 2mcg, Calcium 735mg, Iron 2mg, Potassium 732mg

Hidden Kale Smoothie

Preparation time: 5 minutes

Servings 2

Ingredients:

- 1 medium ripe banana, peeled and sliced
- ½ cup frozen mixed berries
- 1 tbsp hulled hemp seeds
- 2 cups frozen or fresh kale
- 2/3 cup 100% pomegranate juice
- 2¼ cups filtered water

Directions:

1. Add all ingredients in a blender and blend until smooth.
2. Take out and serve.

Nutrition:

Calories 164, Total Fat 2g, Saturated Fat 0.2g, Cholesterol 0mg, Sodium 51mg, Total Carbohydrate 34.2g, Dietary Fiber 3.9g, Total Sugars 17.7g, Protein 4.1g, Vitamin D 0mcg, Calcium 124mg, Iron 2mg, Potassium 776mg

Blueberry Protein Shake

Preparation time: 5 minutes

Servings 1

Ingredients:

- ½ cup cottage cheese
- 3 tbsp vanilla protein powder
- ½ cup frozen blueberries
- ½ tsp maple extract
- ¼ tsp vanilla extract
- 2 tsp flaxseed meal
- Sweetener, choice
- 10-15 ice cubes
- ¼ cup water

Directions:

1. Add all ingredients in a blender and blend until smooth.
2. Take out and serve.

Nutrition:

Calories 559, Total Fat 4.2g, Saturated Fat 1.9g, Cholesterol 14mg, Sodium 659mg, Total Carbohydrate 31.1g, Dietary Fiber 4.5g, Total Sugars 20.7g, Protein 98g, Vitamin D 0mcg, Calcium 518mg, Iron 3mg, Potassium 676mg

Raspberry Lime Smoothie

Preparation time: 5 minutes

Servings 2

Ingredients:

- 1 cup water
- 1 cup fresh or frozen raspberries
- 1 large frozen banana
- 2 tbsp fresh juice, lime
- 1 tsp oil, coconut
- 1 tsp agave

Directions:

1. In a blender put all ingredients and blend until smooth.
2. Take out and serve

Nutrition:

Calories 227,Total Fat 4g, Saturated Fat 1.3g, Cholesterol 0mg, Sodium 7mg, Total Carbohydrate 47.8g, Dietary Fiber 6g, Total Sugars 40.7g, Protein 0.9g, Vitamin D 0mcg, Calcium 22mg, Iron 1mg, Potassium 144mg

Peppermint Monster Smoothie

Preparation time: 5 minutes

Servings 1

Ingredients:

- 1 large frozen banana, peeled
- 1½ cups non-dairy milk
- A handful of fresh mint leaves, stems removed
- 1-2 handfuls spinach

Directions:

1. Add all ingredients in a blender and blend until smooth.
2. Take out and serve

Nutrition:

Calories 799, Total Fat 28.1g, Saturated Fat 16.7g, Cholesterol 110mg   , Sodium 645mg, Total Carbohydrate 98.4g, Dietary Fiber 4.5g, Total Sugars 77.2g, Protein 46.2g,   Vitamin D 7mcg, Calcium 1634mg, Iron 2mg, Potassium 1366mg

Amazing Blueberry Smoothie

Preparation time: 5 minutes

Servings 2

Ingredients:

- ½ avocado
- 1 cup frozen blueberries
- 1 cup raw spinach
- ¼ tsp sea salt
- 1 cup soy
- 1 frozen banana

Directions:

1. Blend everything in a powerful blender until you have a smooth, creamy shake.
2. Enjoy your healthy shake and start your morning on a fresh note!

Nutrition:

Calories 269, Total Fat 12.3g, Saturated Fat 2.3g, Cholesterol 0mg, Sodium 312mg, Total Carbohydrate 37.6g, Dietary Fiber 8.2g, Total Sugars 22.9g, Protein 6.4g, Vitamin D 0mcg, Calcium 52mg, Iron 3mg, Potassium 528mg

The 'Green Machine' Smoothie

Preparation time: 3 minutes

Servings 2

Ingredients

- 1 cup spinach
- ½ cup broccoli
- 2 Sticks of Celery
- 4 tbsp desiccated coconut
- 1 banana
- 1 scoop vegan unflavored protein powder
- 1 cup almond milk
- 1 cupwater

Directions:

1. Pop everything in a blender and blitz
2. Pour into glasses and serve.

Nutrition:

Calories 780, Total Fat 66.5g, Saturated Fat 57.9g, Cholesterol 0mg, Sodium 224mg, Total Carbohydrate 38.8g, Dietary Fiber 15g, Total Sugars 18.4g, Protein 19.6g, Vitamin D 0mcg, Calcium 82mg, Iron 5mg, Potassium 1108mg

Go-Green Smoothie

Preparation time: 5 minutes

Servings 1

Ingredients:

- 2 tablespoons, natural cashew butter
- 1 ripe banana
- 2/3 cup, unsweetened coconut
- ½ cup kale

Directions:

1. Put everything inside a powerful blender.
2. Blend until you have a smooth, creamy shake.
3. Enjoy your special green smoothie.

Nutrition:

Calories 500, Total Fat 33.2g, Saturated Fat 18.9g, Cholesterol 0mg, Sodium 161mg, Total Carbohydrate 48.6g, Dietary Fiber 10.4g, Total Sugars 19.8g, Protein 9.1g, Vitamin D 0mcg, Calcium 72mg, Iron 9mg, Potassium 777mg

Banana Green Smoothie

Preparation time: 5 minutes

Servings 1

Ingredients:

- 1 cup coconut water
- ¾ cup plant-based milk
- ¼ tsp vanilla extract
- 1 heaping cup loosely packed spinach
- 2-3 cups frozen bananas, sliced

Directions:

Blend everything until smooth and serve.

Nutrition:

Calories 364, Total Fat 4.8g, Saturated Fat 2.6g, Cholesterol 15mg, Sodium 111mg, Total Carbohydrate 78g, Dietary Fiber 8g, Total Sugars 45.1g, Protein 9.6g, Vitamin D 1mcg, Calcium 257mg, Iron 1mg, Potassium 1241mg

Cinnamon Coffee Shake

Preparation time: 5 minutes

Servings 2

Ingredients:

- 1 cup cooled coffee, regular or decaf
- ¼ cup almond or non-dairy milk
- A few pinches cinnamon
- 2 tbsp hemp seeds
- Splash vanilla extract
- 2 frozen bananas, sliced into coins
- Handful of ice

Directions:

1. Chill some coffee in a sealed container for a couple of hours (or overnightbefore making this smoothie, or be ready to use more ice.

2. Add the non-dairy milk, cinnamon, vanilla, and hemp seeds to a blender and blend until smooth. Add the coffee and cut bananas and keep blending until smooth.

3. Add the ice and keep blending on high until there are no lumps remaining. Taste for sweetness and add your preferred plant-based sugar or sugar alternative.

4. Transfer to a glass and serve.

Nutrition:

Calories 197, Total Fat 6.4g, Saturated Fat 0.6g, Cholesterol 0mg, Sodium 5mg, Total Carbohydrate 31.3g, Dietary Fiber 5.2g, Total Sugars 15.8g, Protein 4g, Vitamin D 0mcg, Calcium 53mg, Iron 1mg, Potassium 582mg

Orange Smoothie

Preparation time: 5 minutes

Servings 2

Ingredients:

- 1 cup orange slices
- 1 cup mango chunks
- 1 cup strawberries, chopped
- 1 cup coconut water
- Pinch freshly grated ginger
- 1-2 cups crushed ice

Directions:

Place everything in a blender, blend, and serve.

Nutrition:

Calories 269, Total Fat 12.3g, Saturated Fat 2.3g, Cholesterol 0mg, Sodium 312mg, Total Carbohydrate 37.6g, Dietary Fiber 8.2g, Total Sugars 22.9g, Protein 6.4g, Vitamin D 0mcg, Calcium 52mg, Iron 3mg, Potassium 528mg

Turmeric Smoothie

Preparation time: 5 minutes

Servings 2

Ingredients:

- 2 cups non-dairy milk like coconut, almond
- 2 medium bananas, frozen
- 1 cup mango, frozen
- 1 tsp turmeric, ground grated, peeled
- 1 tsp fresh ginger, grated, peeled
- 1 tbsp chia seeds
- ¼ tsp vanilla extract
- ¼ tsp cinnamon, ground
- 1 pinch pepper, ground

Directions:

Blend all ingredients in a blender and serve

Nutrition:

Calories 785, Total Fat 62.4g, Saturated Fat 51.5g, Cholesterol 0mg, Sodium 41mg, Total Carbohydrate 60.2g, Dietary Fiber 15g, Total Sugars 33.9g, Protein 10g, Vitamin D 0mcg, Calcium 149mg, Iron 6mg, Potassium 1292mg

Very Berry Smoothie

Preparation time: 5 minutes

Servings 2

Ingredients:

- 2 cups, plant-based Milk
- 2 cups, Frozen or fresh berries
- ½ cup Frozen ripe bananas
- 2 teaspoons, Flax Seeds
- ¼ tsp, Vanilla
- ¼ tsp, Cinnamon

Directions:

1. Mix together milk, flax seeds, and fruit. Blend in a high-power blender.
2. Add cinnamon and vanilla. Blend until smooth.
3. Serve and enjoy!

Nutrition:

Calories 269, Total Fat 12.3g, Saturated Fat 2.3g, Cholesterol 0mg, Sodium 312mg, Total Carbohydrate 37.6g, Dietary Fiber 8.2g, Total Sugars 22.9g, Protein 6.4g, Vitamin D 0mcg, Calcium 52mg, Iron 3mg, Potassium 528mg

Coco Loco Smoothie

Preparation Time: 5 minutes

Servings: 2

Ingredients

- Coconut milk: 1 cup
- Frozen cauliflower florets: ½ cup
- Frozen mango cubes: 1 cup
- Almond butter: 1 tbsp

Directions:

1. Add all the ingredients to the blender
2. Blend on high speed to make it smooth

Nutrition:

Carbs: 18.2 g

Protein: 10.2 g

Fats: 27.0 g

Calories: 309 Kcal

Creamy Carrot Smoothie

Preparation Time: 5 minutes

Servings: 4

Ingredients

- Almond milk: 2 cups
- Prunes: 60 g
- Banana: 1
- Carrots: 150 g
- Walnuts: 30 g
- Ground cinnamon: ½ tsp
- Vanilla extract: 1 tsp
- Ground nutmeg: ¼ tsp

Directions:

1. Add all the ingredients to the blender
2. Blend on high speed to make it smooth

Nutrition:

Carbs: 14.9 g

Protein: 3 g

Fats: 4.5 g

Calories: 103 Kcal

Pumpkin Smoothie

Preparation time: 5 minutes

Servings 2

Ingredients:

- 1 cup unsweetened non-dairy milk
- 2 medium bananas, peeled and cut into quarters and frozen
- 2 medjool dates, pitted
- 1 cup pumpkin puree, canned or fresh
- 2 cups ice cubes
- ¼ tsp cinnamon
- 2 tbsp ground flaxseeds
- 1 tsp pumpkin spice

Directions:

Blend all ingredients in a blender and serve.

Nutrition:

Calories 272, Total Fat 5.6g, Saturated Fat 2.2g, Cholesterol 10mg, Sodium 75mg, Total Carbohydrate 51.9g, Dietary Fiber 9.5g,Total Sugars 29.4g, Protein 8.2g, Vitamin D 1mcg, Calcium 204mg, Iron 4mg,Potassium 865mg

Date Chocolate Smoothie

Preparation Time: 5 minutes

Servings: 2

Ingredients

- Unsweetened cocoa powder: 2 tbsp
- Unsweetened nut milk: 2 cups
- Almond butter: 2 tbsp
- Dried dates: 4 pitted
- Frozen bananas: 2 medium
- Ground cinnamon: ¼ tsp

Directions:

1. Add all the ingredients to the blender
2. Blend to form a smooth consistency

Nutrition:

Carbs: 72.1 g

Protein: 8 g

Fats: 12.7 g

Calories: 385 Kcal

Date Banana Pistachio Smoothie

Preparation Time: 5 minutes

Servings: 4

Ingredients

- Pistachios: 1 cup
- Raw pumpkin:175 g
- Cloves:1
- Nutmeg:1/8 tsp
- Dates: 4
- Banana:1
- Ground ginger:1/8 tsp
- Ground cinnamon:1 tsp
- Cashew milk:500 ml
- *Ice:* as per your need

Directions:

1. Add all the ingredients to the blender
2. Blend on high speed to make it smooth

Nutrition:

Carbs: 32.9 g

Protein: 9.7 g

Fats: 15 g

Calories: 320 Kcal

Fall Green Smoothie

Preparation Time: 5 minutes

Servings: 1

Ingredients

- Persimmon: 1
- Spinach: 1 cup
- Orange: 1
- Water: 1 cup
- Chia seeds:1 tbsp

Directions:

1. Add all the ingredients to the blender
2. Blend to form a smooth consistency
3. Add ice cubes from the top to chill it

Nutrition:

Carbs: 37.1 g

Protein: 6.5 g

Fats: 5.4 g

Calories: 183 Kcal

Fig Protein Smoothie

Preparation Time: 5 minutes

Servings: 1

Ingredients

- Fresh figs: 2
- Almond milk: 1 cup
- Dried date: 1 pitted
- Vanilla extract: ¼ tsp
- Sesame seeds: 2 tbsp

Directions:

1. Add all the ingredients to the blender
2. Blend to form a smooth consistency

Nutrition:

Carbs: 66.0 g

Protein: 16.1 g

Fats: 18 g

Calories: 435 Kcal

Veggie Smoothie

Preparation time: 10 minutes

Servings 1

Ingredients:

- 1 stalk celery
- 1 carrot peeled and roughly chopped
- ½ cup broccoli sprouts
- 1 cup kale, chopped
- ½ cup curly parsley
- ½ tomato roughly chopped
- ½ avocado
- 1 banana
- ½ green apple
- ½ cup non-dairy milk
- 1 tbsp chia seeds
- 1 tbsp flaxseeds

Directions:

1. Place all ingredients in a blender.
2. Blend until smooth. Serve immediately.

Nutrition:

Calories 696, Total Fat 34.1g, Saturated Fat 7g, Cholesterol 10mg, Sodium 190mg, Total Carbohydrate 90.5g, Dietary Fiber 29.5g, Total Sugars 37.2g, Protein 18.5g, Vitamin D 1mcg, Calcium 527mg, Iron 9mg, Potassium 2223mg

CPSIA information can be obtained
at www.ICGtesting.com
Printed in the USA
BVHW061622020321
601493BV00002B/52